THE LAST WILL & TESTAMENT OF THE UNITED STATES OF AMERICA

ARCHIVE ZERO

ARCHIVE ZERO | NEW YORK | 2020

www.archivezero.com

Published by Archive Zero, LLC

Hardback ISBN: 978-1-7346603-3-3
Paperback ISBN: 978-1-7346603-4-0
E-book ISBN: 978-1-7346603-5-7

Cover design by Robson Garcia Jr.
Formatting by Polgarus Studio.

This poetic work is based on true historic events.

INTRODUCTION

I am a Black Man. I am a Mexican. I am an American. I am a Human.

THIS COLLECTION OF POEMS conveys my anger and sadness over the current state of America—black, brown, yellow, red, white, and blue.

On May 25, 2020—Memorial Day—a white woman named Amy Cooper walked her dog without a required leash in an area of Central Park known as the Ramble, and Christian Cooper, a peaceful, bird watching black man, asked her to leash her dog. The legacy of slavery writ-large in the astounding fact they had the same surname. Amy responded by calling 911 to say that "an African-American man" was threatening her and her dog. Christian calmly recorded the incident. (Imagine what might have happened if he hadn't.) The video went viral and provided a painful reminder of the tradition of white women falsely accusing black men of a crime.

Later that night, in Minneapolis, Minnesota, a black man named George Floyd, who was not resisting arrest, was pressed face down into the pavement with a knee to his neck for seven minutes and 46 seconds—*seven minutes and 46 seconds*—by white Minneapolis police officer Derek Chauvin. Floyd died as he narrated his own death. "I can't breathe." Protests over Floyd's killing raged in cities across America for days, weeks...*forever?*

On July 17, John Lewis, civil rights icon and Georgia Congressman, died from pancreatic cancer, and a few days before he passed, he wrote an essay to be released on the day of his funeral. On July 30, it ran in *The New York Times*. In his essay, Lewis wrote: "When you see something that is not right, you must say something. You must do something."

The Last Will & Testament of the United States of America is my saying and doing "something."

Kelvin C. Bias
Brooklyn, NY
Sept. 1, 2020

CONTENTS

THE LAST WILL & TESTAMENT OF THE UNITED STATES OF AMERICA

GEORGE FLOYD

I bet he liked ice cream.
A young boy, a teen, a man.
Dark skin dripping beneath
A Houston sun. Sky open:
Dreams penetrate the soul.

I bet he liked to dream,
To wander endlessly in
The realm of hope and love,
Trying to peel the yoke of slavery
From his black body.

I bet he liked to smile,
Whoop and holler with
His friends after scoring
A touchdown: Houston Yates.
Third Ward aspirations, big like Texas.

I bet he liked to do what
He had to do, to keep his
Goals alive. Minneapolis.
New dreams, in a new city.
6'4": he is not an invisible man.

I bet he is more than a color.
Yet, in America, black first,
Ask questions later. A gentle giant,
He protected people from harm,
Bouncing, laughing, badly dancing.

I bet he liked to tell stories.
His words linger in the cruel
Holiday air. A spiral of constriction
At the base of an oppressive knee.
"I'm about to die."

THE COOPERS

Meet the Coopers.
They're not a modern
Stone Age family.
It's not a sitcom.
There is no laugh track.

How can it be they
Share a surname?
The legacy of slavery
Gone viral amid a virus.
Amy and Christian.

One walking a dog
Without a leash.
One watching birds
While black, Harvard-bred.
A morning encounter.

The most heinous
Memorial Day is a memory.
Forget? No way.
Racism in the a.m.
Racism in the p.m.

Streets burning in the night.
America's plight. We cry.
There is no theme song.
No national anthem.
Just tears and calls to action.

RED BLOOD, YELLOW PISS

America, the gutter is filling up.
Like a madman drunk on moonshine.

Some Dixie concoction, to block,
Cajole, break the dam of sanity.

I ain't wearing a damn mask.
Others pointing guns at the others,

Do they have anything better to do? ︿
Conceal and carry, follow the deluge,

The water flows to the sea,
Slinging dirt, poisoning the Gulf,

Widening the gulf between us.
We all have red blood, yellow piss.

SILENT BLOOD

Polled and pooled,
Can you hear us bleeding?
The streets vomit rage,
Suckle on division,
Create Confederate collusion.

We're all red when the
Organs seep. Deep state?
More like deep hate.
And the war on drugs
Means brown people in cages.

When long lines at the voting
Place is a weapon of bad taste.
Look to Lady Liberty on her side,
Beaten by a federal soldier's baton,
Chicago, Portland, Albuquerque.

'68 redux, democracy in flux.
If you can't win, shut down the
Post office. Must be too many
Brown faces there, too many
Valid votes you don't like.

Shame, shame, shame.
In a name: duplicitous treason.
Line your pockets, animus complete.
The United States of America:
Find your pulse before it's too late.

AMERICAN HERO

We walk the city at night.
Safe in the notion we get
From watching too many
Superhero movies. We don't
Have our own theme music.
Stagnant cords of discord
Replaced them long ago.

Yet we still believe our
System is the best.
We think someone will
Step from the shadows
To save us. Lift us up
When our bodies rot,
Bullets shot. Fathoms

Of darkness, tears, shocks,
The masked man with
A smile on his face.
We think, even as our light fades,
He will come. He will save the day.
He will step in. But he won't.
He'll simply step on your neck.

VIOLATION OF HUMANITY

"They'll kill me. They'll kill me."
Dying last words uploaded
To the street. They happened.
How many times can you say,
I can't breathe? Over 20.

Basic human understanding,
Basic human compassion,
Basic human explanation?
There isn't one. No logic.
Just an unjust violation of humanity.

How many breaths does the
Average cop breathe when
He puts you in a chokehold,
Clubs you with a baton, puts
A knee on your neck? 8 minutes.

Living words of an officer
Creeping toward a cell:
"Stop talking, stop yelling,
It takes a heck of a lot
Of oxygen to talk."

How much oxygen did you
Need to utter those words?
Those callous syllables,
Those inhuman gerunds.
We'll be "talking" forever.

I COULD STAND NAKED ON THE CORNER OF 57TH & SEVENTH

I could stand naked on the corner
Of 57th & Seventh.
I could, but "Karen" would
Call the cops on me,
Her name the same, greater
Than my slave name.

I could stand naked on the corner
Of 57th and Seventh. I could, but
I might have an eight-minute knee
Wedged in my neck like mineral spirits.
Posters and protests.
"I can't breathe."

I could stand naked on the corner
Of 57th and Seventh.
But I could get shot 41 times.
I could have a Harvard degree,
But I would be threatening,
Looking for birds.

I could stand naked on the corner
Of 57th & Seventh. But I
Wouldn't be painted.
I would choke on fumes,
Suspicious-looking.
Plein air, America.

WHERE IS OUR LEADER?

Red, red, red, blood and flames,
Flashes of fury in a free land.
Bravery is out the window.
What do you do when the
First responders kill you?
Orange frenzy, oozing lies,
When the looting starts,
The shooting starts?

Zoom in on a fireball.
Zoom. Zoom. Zoom.
Talk about it. What do you see?
The hatred, the impossibility
Of healing, Minneapolis, New York,
Atlanta, L.A., D.C.
Where is our leader?
Fearless, American Dictator.

Loser of the popular vote.
A poplar planter in dark skies.
Obama? Biden?
McConnell? Working on their
Dueling conclusions.
Outside agitators. No.
Citizens like, you and me.
Skeletons waving flags.

Masked marauders,
Tears in gas, guzzled,
Siphoned, shot into the air.
Flash bombs.
Snap, crackle, pop.
Breaking news,
Breaking news,
Breaking news.

Grab your poker.
Stir hope, pour love
On the fire. Fingers
On the triggers.
The Constitution
Smolders. Tanks, let's see.
And a charred carcass
For unequal measure.

THE AMERICAN FLAG
NEVER CALLED ME A NIGGA

The American flag can't speak.
But if she could, what would she say?
Would there be an ode to Betsy?
Or a cry of rage, done in her name?

Francis Scott doesn't hold the key,
He championed slavery, smiled at three-fifths.
Muhammad Ali, born Cassius, Louisville,
Didn't float to have fellow Americans

Call him a nigga. Then sit behind a mic.
And refuse to go to Vietnam, saying on point:
"They never called me a nigga."
"They never lynched me."

It's called whitewashing for a reason.
Those in power scrub the books,
Erase marks they don't want you to see.
Cook against the alleged men of Cain.

Red, white, and blue. Beautiful. Three colors,
Three hundred thirty million hues.
The American flag never called me a nigga,
But...

MINNEHAHA

Bloodshot sky, bloodshot flames.
Embers in every direction,
Except justice. The last light
Of spring, preparation for a
Summer burning of marches.

Eyes televised to the fires,
Shapes running in the dark,
Heads bobbing. Mass action.
In the searing sunset, a sign
Marred by smoke: Minnehaha.

An avenue, not a bad American
Joke. Green sign with white letters,
Our nation hanging in the balance.
Remembrance is a visceral thing.
And we're all choking.

COMMERCIAL DAISY

Flowers and tweeting birds.
Petals plucked, discarded.
What do we have to say to
A miscounting little girl?
I don't want to go into the dark.
I want the sun to shine, to rise
On a new day, a new government.
My daughters want to pick daisies,
Film a commercial, smile with her,
Without fear of America's death knell.

When does the anti-democracy
Countdown begin, obscene bombs
Destined for black and white film?
If we are all God's children,
Must we love? Must we try?
Zoom into the twinkling eye.
There's only one thing to do:
You must vote or you *will* die.
The stakes are too high for
You to stay home.

PATRIOT

The word "patriot" bites.

Patriot Missiles,
Patriot Act,
We're "Patriots",
You're "un-American."

We Cannot Stay Silent About:
The Patriot Act.

We Cannot Stay Silent About:
The Word "Patriot"
Being a Euphemism for
"White Nationalist."

We Cannot Stay Silent About:
People Exercising their
Second Amendment Rights (Riots)
Being Called "GREAT PATRIOTS!" and
People Exercising First Amendment Rights
Being Called "Libtards" and "Snowflakes."
The divide is our undoing.
Avoid a New Civil War.

We Cannot Stay Silent.
Patriotism is Shouting
From the Mountaintop.

THE CLOWN

The buffoon hides his antic tasks with
A white mask and shiny frills.
Gaggles of opposition giggles reset his
Internal clock of dueling jests,

Chest bouncing in the air on a blue
Trampoline suit. Catching zest and zeal
Greater than millions of heartbeats tapped.
A string of 7s in line.

Joker's Wild. Hate, time after time.
Inside the laugh, there is no sign.
Just the delicate fancies of a newborn child
High on the flying trapeze. He lies.

Kissing the sky and Cloud No. 9,
The father of uncalculated nonsense
And unrelenting orange hair,
Performs tricks in the early morning haze.

VOTE

Don't stand still,
The sidelines are not your friend.
Your friends are dying, crying,
Trying to refrain from despair.
Strike your hand, rise,
Pull the lever,
Punch the screen,
Fill an Oval.
The revolution starts there.
And America thanks you.

MATTHEW HENSON

A black face in a white world.
Standing atop the globe.
Stark dark hands in a polar swirl.
Magnetic, fierce, skilled.
He could breathe in the cold air well.

Peary's right hand man.
Yet the first one on the ice.
The first of the non-natives.
Was there an ulterior motive?
A white man's unspoken fear?

Explore. Supposedly no.
But we don't write the history books.
He was forgotten for years.
Now we're all Matthew Henson
And the ice looks a little thin.

I BELIEVE IN UNICORNS

I believe things can change.
I believe the future is unwritten.
I believe the carnage of war
Will end one day, and a new war
Will be fought with sticks and stones.

Will the better angels overcome nature?
I believe the odds are pending,
A clock feuding with its own gears,
There's no sense in winding.
I believe in unicorns too.

THE PRISON IN 10 SCENES

I.

One out of every three
Black boys born today
Can expect to be
Sentenced to prison.[1]

II.

What will you do to prevent
The incarceration of a nation?
The slide into oblivion.
End uneven drug sentences.

III.

The prison is in our minds,
The looking the other way,
Crossing to the other side
Of the street. Mind in retreat.

IV.

We shall come over and be free.
We shall walk across the bridge,
Shining paths to the golden shore.
We are in this together.

V.

Think before you act.
A lifetime for a split second.
Canned rage with your dignity intact.
Let it out inside the voting shack.

VI.

Every citizen should have the right to vote.
Every citizen should exercise it.
The walls are blinded by apathy.
Tear them down in the light.

VII.

We aren't actors. This is real.
Pain, honed with a chisel,
Quarried to erect more division.
Let's work on lifting the curtain.

VIII.

A Black person is five times
More likely to be stopped
Without just cause
Than a white person.[2]

IX.

Build less prisons, build *true* just causes.
The sun doesn't shine in a cell.
No time to sunbathe on the Yard.
America needs a new measurement.

X.

Those in power. You can do better.
The black, white, yellow and brown.
A melting pot, an exalted country,
Invest in glorious paths. Learn.

[1] Source: NAACP Criminal Justice Fact Sheet
[2] Source: NAACP Criminal Justice Fact Sheet

ALL BECAUSE A BLACK MAN
WAS PRESIDENT?

The chips inserted, tracked, jacked,
Manipulated. Keep us down.
Keep us contained.
Shout "fuck you" at the top of our lungs.
Masks? I have a right to infect you.

When was the point of no return,
When democracy died?
Assassinated by a photo-op.
A church operation, a new religion,
Greasing the wheels of martial law.

Impartial? Hell no!
Vote! March! Boycott! Sit-In!
America, thou dost not protest enough.
Circuitry is in motion.
Deeds building a coffin.

The dogs will come for you.
The shotgun killers of joggers.
The teary-eyed conscience of
A non-benevolent officer.
The cameras of the watchers.

Electric strains...o' say can you hear?
A guitar's singular discordance. Liberty,
Do your bloody fingers need a plectrum?

It is your patriotic duty not to follow
A would-be emperor, obese on lies.

Overturn the insidious legislation
Proffered by flag-waving bodies of
Lawmakers drunk on fascism.
The Squad, progressives, fight the
Fires with the antidote of resistance.

But remember the chips, wary.
They know where you are.
Anyone who can read is a target,
Anyone who knows the Constitution.
The rights the right squeezes.

A sea of angry faces wrapped in
Red, white, and blue. It's our flag,
But not for you. I'll show you
While I guzzle gas and pizza.
The minority will be the majority.

This creeping fear, this hallowed
Nation, crumbling, raging, divided.
We need love of reason, love of
Egalitarian goals without treason.
We need a televised revolution.

Fight facts, build supermax, fuel the super
Storms, the storm troopers (super duper!),
The majority fears becoming a minority.
Trade those rights, cage the intellectuals!
All because a black man was President?

IN THIS CITY THE DOORS
ARE ALWAYS UNLOCKED

In this city the doors are always unlocked,
And love is a benevolent prowler.
Doubts, hate, voter suppression,
Cast aside, faster than wildfire.
We dream in open halls of power,
Where demagoguery is outlawed.

In this city the doors are always unlocked,
And democracy is alert, a growing child.
It isn't chained away in the basement,
Overturned by subterfuge and greed.
We lust for no need of destruction,
A land where The Hill works well.

In this city the doors are always unlocked,
And everyone has what they need.
Freedoms, not antagonistic fiefdoms,
Abound and multiply: peace is found.
We no longer have a need for
Hounds and blood.

EXCITED DELIRIUM

He looked dangerous.
Face down in the pavement,
Handcuffed. Life on a countdown.
There will be no Mars launch.
The trembling anger at the outcome
Simmers in the long summer.
Psychiatrists, doctors, WHO:
It doesn't exist. The racism does.
The boiling point became boilerplate.
Excited delirium? Whatever.

AMERICA IS BURNING

America, who lit the fuse?
The architects of three-fifths?
The military industrial complex,
The fits of rage at rallies,
The red-hatted minions, the
Creator of seven shots in the back?

The shells of automobiles reek of fuel.
The strains of mine eyes have seen...
The words escape me. Forgotten.
Or never learned?
Freedom of religion? Or freedom
To use religion to abuse?

There are enough reasons to be angry.
Sadness reigns. Keeping wrath at bay.
What does it take to love a country?
Following orders from those who spew hate?
Wondering wherein love is directed.
Players do more than dribble.

A democratic nation, mud washed,
Applied to the eyes.
Red Georgia clay cleansed.
Let the wisdom rise from the
Pool of Siloam as we now
See the embers never fade.

JOHN LEWIS

The boy from Troy
Was always a man,
Walked across a bridge,
Built many, he's still walking,
He's still marching,
He's still fair housing,
Still legislating non-violence.

His eyes are the conscience
Of a nation, reparation.
The road *still* lies ahead.
We cannot stop.
We cannot lose faith.
We have miles to go,
And we shall overcome.

FATHOMS OF BLACKNESS

The first depth sears like a black cauldron
That nobody dares to see, skin lucid,
Crying, pointing to injustice,
Then walloped; the victims call it
The Black Moth, the seething rage,
Anchored in testimonials of slaves,
The forgotten soldiers, descendants
Of Gorée, placated by cries of "it
Will be different this time", while
The eyes of the perpetrator deny.

The second depth transcends death,
Allowing no pain to sink into the soil,
No souls saturated with unused knowledge
From books, from the triumphant words,
Bent, skewed and misaligned in
"Disproportionate numbers", spun on
Rain-slicked Hefty bags atop rock-strewn
Lawns after the fair neighbors escaped
Long ago; no one wants to see it
On the news, writ dark, and darker.

The third depth sets the focus,
Beyond the assassins' bullets: '63, '65,
Two in '68, burn, baby, burn, rise
Reborn of the ashes stirred and
Wiped away like nightsticks, the firms
And firmaments have to be on our side,

Benign in their embrace, insidious
In their targeted transfer to other pleasures,
The plants, husked and smoked, it
Can't be the only way to get ahead.

The fourth is synthetic flesh, impervious,
Blacker than the night crossing, blacker
Than the hearts who created three-fifths,
The ridiculous pantheon of the ages,
Hallways certain among us will never walk,
Tread upon the roads we helped build.
Banneker, and his plans, the district of
Tomorrow, the hope, yes, we can, we can
And will, standing above the light,
Steeled in our once submerged blackness.

The fifth and final fathom: a portal for piers
Filled with portmanteaus and poets, the
Countrymen of all colors, brown, beige,
Yellow, chocolate, milk, coronas of white,
Ascending with the elevating oceans,
We float together in a pool of knowing,
Undeterred, dreams not deferred,
Haggling amendments hashed out, grins,
Votes cast, water rushing into the
Gutter, where we gnash our white teeth.

THE LAST WILL & TESTAMENT OF
THE UNITED STATES OF AMERICA

I.

I, the United States of America,
Residing mainly in North America,
Planet Earth, in the Milky Way Galaxy,
Being of sound and disposing mind
And Congress body, do hereby make
And declare this to be my
Last Will & Testament,
Revoking all prior Wills and Codicils.

II.

Identification of Family:
I have a wife; her name is Lady Liberty.
She cries tears of blood.
I have untold millions of children.
Sons and daughters, dead, alive,
Indifferent, numb to the pain,
Killed in foreign wars in faraway lands,
Killed on my soiled body, the shackles of slaves.

III.

I NOMINATE, CONSTITUTE and APPOINT
The survivors, the minions of love, and
Disciples of Dr. Martin Luther King,
The angels of democratic policy, and proponents
Of universal health care and a living wage,
To be the Estate Trustees, Executors, and
Trustees of this, my Will. The People,
Adherents to the creed, willing to execrate hate.

IV.

Trustees of my Will, my estate,
Or portion thereof, who may be acting
As such from time to time whether
Original or substituted and whether one or more.
I request that no Executor, Trustee
Or successor in such capacity,
Or any other fiduciary hereunder,
Shall be allowed to profit from war.

V.

Disinheritance:
Those who legislate hate,
Stoke the fires of pain,
Look at themselves in the Twitter
Mirror in vain. The complicit.
The dark stains of inhumanity,
The mistletoe burners, and their
Ilk. You get nothing: scorched Earth.

VI.

Payment of Debts:
There will be no independent inquiry.
The truth flees. Debts of blood,
Forgiven. I, America, should
Always pay my debts.
Birth of a Nation, KKK,
John Wilkes Booth.
Black bodies beaten and slain.

VII.

Payment of Taxes:
I owe no taxes, but a hell
Of a lot of refunds.
Fecund times wasted
In the belly of nuclear beasts.
Blinding heat, transferred guilt.
If you foment division,
A million times more.

VIII.

Property to Trustees:
All indigenous Americans,
The named and the unnamed,
Among them: Blackfoot, Sioux,
Iroquois, Arapaho, Navajo.
Nez Perce, Apache, Comanche.
This land is your land.
It's not my land.

IX.

Distribution of Property:
The golden shores of prosperity
To the poor. The families of the dead.
Emmett Till, Malcolm X, MLK
Trayvon Martin, Eric Garner, Michael Brown,
Tamir Rice, Walter Scott, Freddie Gray,
George Floyd. Too many names.
Not enough reparations.

X.

Funeral Arrangements I:
Service at Toroweap Overlook.
Only close friends and family:
First Peoples and Nations of Peace.
There are to be no tears,
Only borderless shamans,
Smiles, a celebration of life.
If it remains, if it's not oppressed.

XI.

Funeral Arrangements II:
My body will not lie in state.
No sitting or past presidents,
If they are still alive, will be
Allowed to speak. Their voices
Are muted. Your voices are raised.
You, the People, the mindful survivors.
France will give the eulogy.

XII.

Funeral Arrangements III:
The revolution will not be televised.
My ashes will not be spread.
There will be no monument, only memory.
The only trace stone tablets at Trinity Site.
Crafted to be impervious to
Destruction from water or man's folly.
Storytellers will infinitely relay my highest ideas.

XIII.

Funeral Arrangements IV:
No taxpayer money will be used.
Well, there is no money left.
The 1% took it offshore and
Built their border wall.
Rakim's "I Ain't No Joke"
Will be played on a Boombox.
When I'm gone, still no jokes.

XIV.

Burial Stipulations:
No autopsy is to be performed.
Causes of Death: Apathy,
Avarice, Autoeroticism of Hate,
Vulgarity, Charlatanism, Bluster,
Fascism, Nationalism, and Racism.
Let me soil, wither, burn in the sun.
Eolian endgame: let my soul remain.

XV.

Specific Gifts:
I have no more gifts to give.
No more breaths or fresh air.
No more eroded hillsides.
I do leave a legacy of hope.
Of a shining beacon on a hill.
Will you pick up the torch?
You, the survivor, the soldier in the war.

XVI.

Debts, Expenses, and Taxes
Sell democracy to the highest bidder.
To the technocratic aftermath,
The pilloried body of high-minded
Individuals. My debts accrue for eternity.
Sell my gold, my natural resources.
Only pay debts that are just and good,
Created in a solid human condition.

XVII.

Residue:
The burden is on the speaker.
To elevate the discourse,
To shun idioms of brute force
And "heavily-armed" police,
Law and order, division inducing,
My burden is done, for I am no more.
I stand like a ghost. I'm not holy.

XVIII.

Alternate Residue:
The amber waves of grain,
My Country 'Tis Of Thee
Sweet Land of Liberty.
No one sing for me.
Write lyrics of a different sort.
New words encased behind a glass.
If any children linger, teach the Golden Rule.

XIX.

Payments for Minors:
Invest in the youngest among us.
My descendants. Like Liberia.
Manage their mutual love well.
Fiduciary arrangements work best
In the absence of income inequality.
There is no need for courts if
Human rights are adhered to.

XX.

More Possessions:
Take my tears. Take 'em!
The blood on the floor.
The air in the wind.
Gone. Red, white and who?
Who will mourn the bodies?
The unmoored, the unknown.
Let the world see my lacrimation.

XXI.

Possessions of History:
Crispus Attucks. Betsy Ross,
Nathan Hale. Paul Revere.
Solomon Northrop, Oliver North.
Kennedy. Dubya, Nixon too.
Take them all. We all will fall.
Time and chance. We exist.
We persist. I gave it my all.

XXII.

Less Division:
No hateful words.
No Ku Klux Klan crosses,
Crossed in gilded gardens.
Abolish the Confederate flag.
All acts of sedition forgiven if...
If, if, if, if, if. Posse Comitatus.
We all need to be committed.

XXIII.

Nuclear Disarmament:
I have enough nuclear weapons.
Russia has enough. France,
The U.K., China, India, Pakistan,
North Korea, Israel. We all have enough.
You couldn't make do with less?
Perhaps none. What are we
Waiting for? All of us to die too?

XXIV.

Essential Workers:
Listen to the doctors, when it comes
To viral outbreaks, not viral videos,
Those who have medical degrees,
Those who put their lives on the line.
The ones who plug the holes.
Sit back and listen while
You bang your pots and pans.

XXV.

Holding for Minors I:
For the young, I give my
Breath. My determination,
Grace, my better morals,
My upright fight for justice,
My compass pointing to the light,
My bleeding hands in need of healing,
My humility in times of unrest.

XXVI.

Holding for Minors II:
The children bearing children,
The future is yours,
But be wise. Be true.
Don't let the cycle continue.
Don't kill the better tomorrow
By not learning enough
About your world first.

XXVII.

My Record Collection I:
Before I forget, it must be said.
Public Enemy, Aretha Franklin,
Stevie Wonder, Teddy Prendergast,
Samuel Barber, Giorgio Moroder,
Pharrell, Marvin Gaye, Prince,
Rodgers & Hammerstein,
Aerosmith, The Beatles, Run DMC.

XXVIII.

My Record Collection II:
The Four Tops, Diana Ross,
The Jackson 5, Isaac Hayes,
Ladysmith Black Mambazo,
Bob Dylan, Tom Petty, Cher,
James Brown, Justin Timberlake,
Bricktop, Josephine Baker,
Edith Piaf, Rakim, Cole Porter.

XXIX.

My Record Collection III:
L.L. Cool J, Johnny Cash,
Beethoven, Britney Spears,
The Four Tops, Barbra Streisand,
Carly Simon, Beyoncé,
Simon & Garfunkel, Miles Davis,
The Beastie Boys, Usher,
Black Sabbath, J. Lo, The Supremes.

XXX.

My Record Collection IV:
Philip Glass, Vangelis,
Donna Summer, Phil Collins,
Ennio Morricone, De La Soul.
Biggie, Tupac, N.W.A., Dr. Dre.
Donate my vinyl to a young
Musician eager to learn, eager to
"Lift Every Voice and Sing".

XXXI.

Trusts:
All trusts will be dissolved.
The remaining monies
To be distributed to each
Of the reservations, the
Land that is not mine.
And reparations to the
Descendants of slaves.

XXXII.

Power to Sell or Hold:
No one may hold this power.
It is within each individual mind,
Within each individual memory.
The landscape of the brain
Dictates freedom. To each his own,
To each her own, to each their own.
Personal liberation must endure.

XXXIII.

Powers of the Executor I:
Any powers not explicitly stated,
Are to be adjudicated by a true heir
Of Ruth Bader Ginsburg: No one
Falsely installed by a Popular Vote
Losing "president." I insist on
SCOTUS term limits now.
Protect the bodies of Ruth.

XXXIV.

Powers of the Executor II:
When all courts and all Congresses,
And all judges fail, when there is no more Earth.
My final fate will be adjudicated
By the most downtrodden remaining,
Those whose ancestors had their necks
Stepped on and couldn't breathe.
On a new space ship.

XXXV.

Investments:
WHO gets the royalties,
The hard-fought blood money?
Health care will get paid.
All just claims of needless pain
And suffering. Hospitals built,
Temperatures tempered.
Education, a free pillar for all.

XXXVI.

Payments to Charities:
All the gold in Fort Knox
Shall be given to the cause
Of social justice, to free education,
To fund free health care,
To defund corrupt police departments,
To fund the betterment of humanity.
To fund my resurrection.

XXXVII.

Distribution in Kind:
Only to the kind warriors.
The better halves trying to
Make us whole without prejudice.
The letter of the law is written
In invisible ink. Spill it and revise.
I don't want to repeat myself,
But sometimes it's necessary.

XXXVIII.

Redress of Grievances:
The lost tribe, the eternal dead:
Wounded Knee, Sandy Hook,
Those sprayed with water cannons
In Alabama, the wrongfully convicted.
Will have their pleas heard.
If only I could restore life,
For those given life, those who lost it.

XXXIX.

Definition of Indigenous:
More than federally recognized tribes.
They are never-ending, they are ascending.
I had no part in this shame.
I follow a trail of my tears,
Unable to upend legislation.
The taking, the raping, the pillaging.
This land is all your land. Spirits decree.

XL.

Real Estate:
States, Territories, Protectorates,
Each state listed here
May choose to continue but must forfeit
All usage of the name "United States".
I own the trademark, and I
Alone can profit from her truths
And her falsehoods: the brand.

XLI.

Delaware, Dec. 7, 1787:
The first state: state of incorporation.
How high were its hopes?
Wilmington, Dover,
Delmarva, Delaware Bay.
Shop on the Riverfront.
Cross the Delaware.
Lead the way.

XLII.

Pennsylvania, Dec. 12, 1787:
Philadelphia, City of Brotherly Love,
Where it all began,
Once the capital of a young nation,
A nation founded on equal ideas,
Kobe Bryant, Meek Mill, Dr. J.
Rocky, the Steel Curtain,
Forging American branches.

XLIII.

New Jersey, December 18, 1787:
Jersey Shore, Wildwood,
Watch the tram car please.
Summer revelers, Cape May,
The land across the Hudson.
Princeton and presidents.
The academic capability,
Without the culpability.

XLIV.

Georgia, January 2, 1788:
The pines of freedom, Arbery, Arbery,
Land of a free preacher,
Peace his shield, his words
Echoing still, to the red clay,
No hate crimes law; erase the hate symbol,
A resounding echo off Stone Mountain,
The Confederacy is no more.

XLV.

Connecticut, January 9, 1788:
New London didn't quite grow
They way they planned.
Nutmeg destiny. Mystic. Yale.
New Haven. They love to see it all.
Insurance and law. U.S.S. Nautilus,
A submerged nuclear dawn.
18th Amendment be damned.

XLVI.

Massachusetts, February 6, 1788:
Plymouth Rock, we light the way.
Cranberries and Cape Cod,
Boston's Tea Party, remember Attucks,
Shots fired, before they see
The whites of their eyes.
Bunker Hill, or bunkered citizens.
One if by land, two if by sea.

XLVII.

Maryland, April 28, 1788:
Fort McHenry, bombs bursting in air
Francis Scott Key, Taney's boy, read
About him in my tomes, slavery's pro,
Seeing a massive flag in the dark, but
For brown-skinned men, stark, like
Freddie Gray, Black-Eyed Susans,
Black pride: B-more! Elijah, we miss you.

XLVIII.

South Carolina, May 23, 1788:
Fort Sumter, first shots of the war,
The War for Abolition, for Union.
Glory, Glory, Hallelujah.
Charleston's beauty and the past's ghosts
The palmettos asunder in the early morn'
Saturday's Gamecocks, united delight.
Come Wednesday, Why, Dylann, why?

XLIX.

New Hampshire, June 21, 1788:
Live Free or Die? We die anyway.
How about Love Free or Die?
The jingle jangles down the slopes
Of Agiocochook, nobody who was
Here first calls it Mount Washington.
The snows wash me clean,
Live Free and Ask Why.

L.

Virginia, June 25, 1788:
A more telling place and date:
Jamestown, 1619, the White Lion.
I am the "20 and odd."
I am the ones who were
Shackled, then regarded
Three-fifths. Charlottesville,
There are bad people on *one* side.

LI.

New York, July 26, 1788:
Lady Liberty, you stand for me,
You stand for thee, you stand,
When people try to step
On your neck. Ellis Island,
Niagara Falls, citizen denizens,
Waiting to go over in a barrel.
Empire of estates. Rising fate.

LII.

North Carolina, November 21, 1789:
Sir Walter Raleigh has a Blue Ridge view.
A city out of the woods, a state
Where we learned to fly,
And Jordan found his air.
Kill Devil Hills, kill the devil.
Let the wild horses run.
Hatteras lights the way.

LIII.

Rhode Island, May 29, 1790:
Drinking lovers in solidarity
With Connecticut, the 18th
Is of no use for providence.
RISD will make it clean as
We sail away from Newport's
Gilded cages, the Breakers.
And dream of WaterFire.

LIV.

Vermont, March 4, 1791:
Ben & Jerry's, the ice cream
We can all get behind.
The kind we can lick injustice with,
The kind that is kind and rewinds
The folds of social inequity so
Everyone can plainly see,
Everyone can choose their flavor.

LV.

Kentucky, June 1, 1792:
First Saturday in May
Hats and mint juleps.
Do you know Jimmy Winkfield?
Black Master, sleek in the saddle.
Ebony skin, run with the wind.
All the jockeys used to be black.
No matter. Breonna Taylor still wonders.

LVI.

Tennessee, June 1, 1796:
Davy Crockett: King of the "Wild" Frontier.
How many black faces
Lifted their backs, and bent
Their eyes to the sky
For freedom, for recognition?
Tana-see, "The Meeting Place",
Where everyone's a Volunteer.

LVII.

Ohio, March 1, 1803:
Mike Fink, the Riverboat King.
Practical jokes and fighting.
So Ohio, so goes The Nation,
Which nation? Which way?
The Snapping Turtle knows.
He'll fill you with moonshine,
Turn that keel. Power needs to heal.

LVIII.

Louisiana, April 30, 1812:
Purchased in 1803. Thank you, France.
You gave me lots of land.
A price I can never repay.
The descendants please take care.
When the Delta runs dry, so does the land.
Silt carried from my mountainous spine.
Deposited for future riverboat gamblers.

LIX.

Indiana, December 11, 1816:
The Hoosier State. Who's ear?
The Brickyard in a country
Filled with unending roads.
The Mound Builders left us long ago.
Their remains, a gift, or a warning.
Nobody wants to see more tombs.
Bloomington quarries, let's break away.

LX.

Mississippi, December 10, 1817:
What can I say? What wrongs, what rights?
The eyes of the world are always upon you.
Emmett Till, Emmett Till, Emmett Till.
A Confederacy of Confederate flags,
Of people upset at the stigma,
Of people trying to overcome. The
Mighty Mississippi cleans everyone's house.

LXI.

Illinois, December 3, 1818:
Chicago wind. Obama. Land of Lincoln,
The golden nose, the bust
In the Springfield air, befriended by trees.
We try to honor our better angels.
I fight, in death, to honor the Illini.
I fight, in death, to honor the
Freedom of slaves. Thank Honest Abe.

LXII.

Alabama, December 14, 1819:
Talladega, Booker T.,
Martin's church, the Rosa Parks Museum.
Montgomery, Birmingham,
The sweet smell of voting rights,
The sweet smell of overcoming.
The swell of humanity in line,
Marching hand in hand in Selma.

LXIII.

Maine, March 15, 1820:
The seemingly forgotten land
In the northeast. Vacationland.
Lobsters and rocks.
We need Stephen King.
He can write my obituary.
He can terrorize those who
Would choose to do my body harm.

LXIV.

Missouri, August 10, 1821:
The Gateway Arch.
Go west young descendants.
Beyond the Mississippi.
Beyond the Missouri,
Listen to the Fergusons
Of the world. The roots.
Hannibal and Huckleberry Finn.

LXV.

Arkansas, June 15, 1836:
Brown vs. The Board of Education
Little Rock, 1954.
Norman Rockwell inspiration.
A man from Hope.
Brought down by a blowjob.
Forty minutes of hell. What happened?
How many bales of Cotton?

LXVI.

Michigan, January 26, 1837:
Don't tread on your right to get sick and die?
Why, go ahead. Congregate.
But must you gleefully wield your guns?
I'll return to prettier thoughts.
Camp Miniwanca, beautiful dunes.
The most domestic of the Great Lakes.
No reason Flint's water can't be fixed.

LXVII.

Florida, March 3, 1845:
Cape Canaveral, Cape Kennedy.
One in the same. It needs more use,
More dreams to the stars, Mars,
More children looking up in envy.
Space X, X-Women, X-Men.
Don't forget Trayvon.
Stand your ground on racial equality.

LXVIII.

Texas, December 29, 1845:
Remember the Alamo.
Remember Dallas. Triple Underpass.
Forget the Wars of Mass Distraction
In the mind, and followers, of the Texas son.
We need a War on Wars,
A War on Fascism, A War
On the Electoral College.

LXIX.

Iowa, December 28, 1846:
Rows and rows of maize,
In all directions, bisecting
A blue horizon and cotton
Ball puffs of water vapor.
Davenport, the Mississippi,
Hawkeyes and Cyclones,
Your soybeans feed the world.

LXX.

Wisconsin, May 29, 1848:
Glaciated remains, lakes,
Dissected till plains.
Eau Claire. Badgers and snow.
The wind whistles from Green Bay
Where ice is the break of day.
Cecil Cooper, Robin Yount, Paul Molitor.
Brew the right brew. Celebrate.

LXXI.

California, September 9, 1850:
The Golden State, 49ers and pickaxes,
Silver-screen Hollywood dreams.
Western civilization from A to Z,
Every landscape within her borders.
Yet the moguls wash over my ills.
Sex scandals and harassed starlets,
The Hollywood Walk of Shame.

LXXII.

Minnesota, May 11, 1858:
The Land of 10,000 Lakes, not Lakers.
The pit of a man's soul can be
Buried, frozen over in, and by, one.
A man who came from elsewhere,
George Floyd, not at the hands
Of the Purple People Eaters,
But the People Eaters in Blue.

LXXIII.

Oregon, February 14, 1859:
Haystack Rock, Crater Lake.
Sunsets and snowy crests.
Cascading to the Pacific.
Rain, rain, go away.
Ducks and Beavers,
A Civil War. A green horizon where
Frank Herbert conjured Dune.

LXXIV.

Kansas, January 29, 1861:
Bleedin', hell, we don't need any slaves.
Go west, young men.
Free Staters remain in reverence.
Now we're 21st century slaves.
Credit, things take years to pay off:
Health and home on the range.
Where the deer and the antelope play.

LXXV.

West Virginia, June 20, 1863:
Harper's Ferry. John Brown's Raid.
Abolitionist's fury needed today.
New River Gorge Bridge.
America's Bungee jump?
No, a steel span to tomorrow.
Like the World Famous Greenbrier Hotel.
Mountaineers are always free.

LXXVI.

Nevada, October 31, 1864:
The Silver State.
Basin and gun ranges,
Or is it rages?
Remember, what happens in
Vegas, stays in Vegas.
Pull them slots and aim
For your neon dreams.

LXXVII.

Nebraska, March 1, 1867:
Flat stones on the wide-eyed Platte.
Chimney Rock sunsets,
The "I" Formation. Wishbone.
Once a thing. Big Red. Like
Kittie McManus on the cover
Of *Sports Illustrated.*

LXXVIII.

Colorado, August 1, 1876:
Whence the rivers flow from
The spine of my body.
Garden of the Gods, Royal Gorge.
Hailstorms outside of Cortez.
Natural resources, natural beauty.
We need a Rocky Mountain High.
But don't forget the Plains.

LXXIX.

North Dakota, November 2, 1889:
The World's Largest Buffalo Monument.
Fargo. I love the plains in winter.
The endless whiteness.
The endless landscape,
Where I can dream of my Southern
Sister. The grounds of our ancestors.
We will defile no more lands.

LXXX.

South Dakota, November 2, 1889:
The Black Hills, Deadwood.
Four faces on a mountain.
When will Crazy Horse
Join the party? Maybe we
Don't need monuments.
Then no one can blast
Their quarry, their belief.

LXXXI.

Montana, November 8, 1889:
Big Sky Country.
I retire here to see the clouds.
To see the Rockies rise
From the amber waves.
From the ghosts of proud Blackfeet.
The rivers that power me begin here,
Flow to an eternal destination.

LXXXII.

Washington, November 11, 1889:
Mount Rainier, 14,410 feet,
Rising like the plinth of rebirth.
Mount St. Helen's, I love your fire.
The Cascades dream on the Pacific,
The sound of Puget Sound,
Seattle, Pioneer Square, Pike Place,
A Space Needle aims for tomorrow.

LXXXIII.

Idaho, July 3, 1890:
Salmon River. Snake River.
Hell's Canyon, and deer.
Craters of the Moon, lava
Leading us to the places
We will revisit one day.
Grab some Chobani in Twin Falls,
While Sawtooth sings.

LXXXIV.

Wyoming, July 10, 1890:
Hell's Half Acre.
Powder River Basin.
Open Range. Open sky.
We can see the future
In every sunset.
Casper, Cheyenne, Cody.
I want to see Buffalo Bill.

LXXXV.

Utah, January 4, 1896:
The Golden Spike.
Mostly Chinese immigrants,
And the Irish. Give them their due.
Promontory: Prominent history.
Zion, Bryce, Great Salt Lake.
Arches and Bonneville.
The place to go to see true stars.

LXXXVI.

Oklahoma, November 16, 1907:
The terminus. The Trail of Tears.
Tulsa, May 31-June 1, 1921.
Land over land. Dust in the bowl.
Did it clean your sins?
S.E. Hinton, she might know.
Rumble Fish. The Outsiders.
All in a state shaped like a gun.

LXXXVII.

New Mexico, January 6, 1912:
Land of Enchantment and
Anasazi Ancestors.
Ship Rock pointing to the stars,
To the lands of those who come after.
Taos hums along. Abiquiú,
Georgia O'Keefe's skulls
A reminder, death stalks us all.

LXXXVIII.

Arizona, February 14, 1912:
By the time I left Arizona,
Grand Canyon State of Mind.
Mindful law and order.
Not Sheriff Joe. I got my
Martin Luther King Jr. Holiday.
Tucson skies, Nogales Highway.
Walls will not unite us.

LXXXIX.

Alaska, January 3, 1959:
Land of the Midnight Sun,
Where you can see Russia
From your house. Oh dear.
Oil fields and Denali,
The true name, the greater.
Glaciers, the Inuit, will they survive
Atop, and at the end, of the world?

XC.

Hawaii, August 21, 1959:
The 50th State. Paradise.
A gem in the Pacific,
Like another world.
Another arm of freedom.
North Shore, Mauna Loa,
Mauna Kea, Haleakalā, Waikiki.
Let's surf to a bountiful forever.

XCI.

American Samoa:
The most patriotic
Islands in our nation.
Let them wear a uniform.
Let them smile beneath
Rainmaker Mountain.
In Pago Pago. In the
Middle of a vast ocean.

XCII.

Guam:
They are Americans too.
They live, work, die.
They bleed. Under
A red, white and blue flag.
They are brothers,
Sisters, mothers, fathers.
We are all Chamorro.

XCIII.

Northern Mariana Islands:
From the sandy Saipan shores
To the coral of Mañagaha,
And the turtles of the Grotto.
A commonwealth of clear water,
A commonwealth of beauty.
Fourteen islands, 14 hideaways,
Places to live, places beneath the sky.

XCIV.

Puerto Rico:
Those in power don't
Want you to become a state,
They don't want more blue (*brown*)
Senators. They'll deny.
But that's what they
Really mean. Don't listen to them.
Beautiful island, beautiful people.

XCV.

U.S. Virgin Islands:
Caribbean state of mind,
But not a state. They
Are Americans by birth too.
Saint Croix, Saint John,
Saint Thomas and the rest,
Blessed by warm air.
I could have retired there.

XCVI.

McMurdo Station:
The beacon to the final continent,
The one that determines the future.
Precious water, enough to
Quench the world.
Divvy it up fairly.
Keep empathy and abundance alive.
Water is life. Water is freedom.

XCVII.

Amundsen-Scott South Pole Station:
Will we drill to the center of the world?
Will we ruin the desolate beauty?
Don't let the Resource Wars impinge.
When the Earth finishes cooking,
The new continent will unleash
Her buried secrets. No more ice.
Only unusual fossils, maybe a spaceship.

XCVIII.

National Parks I:
Yellowstone, the first, and all other
National parks, Monuments,
Sanctuaries, Seashores, et al,
Will remain for the
Tillers of the Earth.
Those who come after,
Those writing the obituary.

XCIX.

National Parks II:
I love them all, but some
Need more attention than
Others, some, are seldom tread.
You may read about them,
If they are still extant.
The following are specific
Statements and provisions.

C.

Yellowstone National Park:
Old Faithful. Are you still blowing?
Do your mists transpire to
An audience or do the wisps
Of vapor float beyond the Dome,
Beyond the rivers, lakes and streams.
Up the Canyon destined for another
Country, another Nation's parks?

CI.

Devil's Tower National Monument:
Close Encounters of the Majestic Kind,
A volcanic plug left long ago,
Still standing in the lands of ancestors.
The first national monument,
But not the last if we keep love green.
Look up to the heavens, the blue sky,
The dawn clouds passing wisdom.

CII.

Arches National Park:
Sunrise, sunset.
Rocks precarious.
Minds in awe. Stars witnesses.
Etchings from eons past,
Eras of free roaming humans.
When no one said:
This is my land.

CIII.

Yosemite National Park:
Pronounce it properly please.
Half Dome & El Capitan.
Pendulum of American beauty.
The Tuolumne River, the trees,
The cascades formed of melting snow.
Our dreams rippling past deer and elk,
Past the residue of grotesquery.

CIV.

Grand Canyon National Park:
Don't desecrate history,
The red layers, the red haze
At sunset. There's not enough
Honor to leave for the ancestors.
The First People who found
This sacred place while
A river ran deep. Muddy and true.

CV.

Crater Lake National Park:
Mount Mazama, the mother,
Nature's pristine architect.
The deepest blue, the deepest
Water. Where is the bottom?
Drive around the Rim.
Ponder the ages of man.
May the Cascades always rise.

CVI.

Great Sand Dunes National Park:
Sangre de Cristo vistas crying
For someone to protect them.
I wait for the spring runoff,
Praying they will continue,
Waiting for the watchers
To allocate more funds to
Keep my creed alive.

CVII.

Glacier National Park:
There used to be trees there,
Two once proud lovers
Forming an X, as if in embrace,
Somewhere near Lake McDonald.
I wonder if they still lean upright,
If the snows keep pace,
And the name isn't Glacial Lakes.

CVIII.

Gateway Arch National Park:
A monument to Westward Expansion,
Or the blood spilled to achieve it?
When nature overtakes humanity,
The Arch might remain true
As descendants ascertain
A new direction from an old relic.
I hope for heightened truths.

CIX.

White Sands National Park:
This is my meditation zone.
Shhh...don't tell anyone.
Get there before dawn, and
You'll have it all to yourself.
The gypsum grains, the white clouds,
And the pink, then orange,
Then blue sky. Catch my eye.

CX.

Sequoia National Park:
The General Sherman Tree.
Slow-motion tracking,
Slow-motion growth,
You've seen the time lapse.
Largest tree on Earth,
Voluminous, altitudinous.
I want her to grow forever.

CXI.

Acadia National Park:
After the last riot burns out,
When the stench of gasoline,
Rage and rifle fire expires,
There is a place I want to
Drive to. Cadillac Mountain.
To fill the time under
The stars in Maine.

CXII.

Everglades National Park:
The gators have their amusement.
We have the Glades. The rangers,
Manatees, panthers, we all play there.
We wait for the morning sun.
To see the glistening panoply.
Anhinga Trail, stand proud,
And elevate able American ideas.

CXIII.

Gates of the Arctic National Park:
North of the Circle; Carter's gift.
Oolah, I'm proud to bear witness here.
Brown bears, and brown earth,
Frozen in time for the future.
The Brooks Range, immortal,
Bedlam for a pedestal of snow,
Paradise for the fauna overtaking man.

CXIV.

Death Valley National Park:
One morning, in the early light,
After the Big One, and oceans surge,
The Panamint Range becomes an island.
Dear Visitor, please ensure
My ideas of democracy and
Freedom of speech endure
As long as the wind-carved dunes.

CXV.

Cape Cod National Seashore:
Do not put Thoreau behind you.
Do not put America behind you.
Remember the shores of Massachusetts.
The rocks, that some landed on,
Others not. But destiny can be changed.
Wellfleet, Truro, Provincetown.
The dunes, the magnificent dunes.

CXVI.

Hovenweep National Monument:
Stones quarried before history,
Before the white man came,
Before smallpox and finite sunsets,
I return this land to the spirits,
The ghosts of those unnamed.
Dark sky spaces retreat into the
Vestiges of a pueblo dweller's dream.

CXVII.

Canyons of the Ancients National Monument:
Nearby, Colorado and Utah never appeared
On their maps. Structures without strictures.
The mesas, tables to the great unknown.
Sandstone, blue sky, red blood,
Dried, yet still remains the same.
Kivas, lone in the midday sun,
Monuments to my progenitors, I am yours.

CXVIII.

Mount Rushmore National Memorial:
Designed by a member of the KKK.
Didn't finish Stone Mountain
To desecrate a piece of stolen land.
Four faces, four different sins.
Many different people's blood spilled.
Many different ways of life converged.
I don't need monuments for I am gone.

CXIX

Statue of Liberty National Monument:
I regress. I need one. One pinnacle
Of hope and independence. Never slaves again.
Racism, the architect of many ills,
The foundation of today's thrills.
If her torch falls, raise freedom,
Not FreeDumb—again.
Relight the word and the world.

CXX.

Los Angeles:
The Lakers, Jack,
Red Hot Chili Peppers.
Smack dab at the edge
Of the Pacific,
Looking westward to
The Far East. Rodney King.
Vote, don't loot.

CXXI.

Chicago:
Skyscrapers rise from
Lake Michigan like giants
Seeking a clean drink.
Jordan and the Bulls.
They live forever.
Obama's acceptance.
Never forget '68.

CXXII.

New York City:
The Big Apple.
Financial District.
Where the ghost of slaves
Still request recompense.
Lady Liberty's Island,
Her hands, her feet.
My memory incomplete.

CXXIII.

Route 66:
From Illinois to California.
Oklahoma, New Mexico.
On to Arizona, sunsets,
Sunrises, this is my road.
When I want to unwind.
When the pressure of
Upholding my citizens fails.

CXXIV.

Settlement of Claims:
I am not a litigator.
I am not a prosecutor.
I am not a defendant.
Though some of my actions
May qualify. I ask forgiveness.
I make no further claims.
Only those outlined herein.

CXXV.

Chinese Exclusion Act of 1882:
They built the Railroad.
The ties that bind, the will of
Thousands, all came crashing
Down with the stroke of
Chester A. Arthur's pen.
Never again.
Inclusion is America's fusion.

CXXVI.

List of the Bereaved I:
The Kennedys: John & Bobby.
Malcolm X and MLK,
Sandy Hook parents,
Vietnam parents,
Vietnamese children,
The good citizens of Flint,
Marvin Gaye's father.

CXXVII.

List of the Bereaved II:
The families of Eric Garner,
Trayvon Martin, Michael Brown,
Sandra Bland, Freddie Gray,
Breonna Taylor, George Floyd,
And scores more, unnamed
And unburied First Peoples,
Beneficiaries of Lincoln.

CXXVIII.

List of the Bereaved III:
Black Wall Street.
Tulsa, Oklahoma.
The shame swept under
The rug of history. Repent, culprits.
And make no acts that deny
Generational black wealth,
Those that killed rightful inheritance.

CXXIX

List of the Bereaved IV:
The Gnadenhutten Massacre,
Tippecanoe, I took their land.
My tears drop on stolen soil.
Mankato Executions, trials,
Retributions. The Sand Creek Massacre:
Bloody, atrocious, a missionary's work?
The Ghost Dancers of Wounded Knee.

CXXX.

Executive Order 9066:
Another dark chapter of my past.
My human citizens: I am guilty.
The root of all evil isn't money:
Fanatical fear of the other.
Lay down your prejudice
At the door of opportunity.
Open your gates and enemies retreat.

CXXXI.

Heart Mountain Internment Camp:
Wyoming, why? Concentrated.
And yes, interned is the term.
Why do the clouds still shed tears?
American families, unfamiliar terrain.
A mountain in the distance,
A place to dream beyond,
A marker in the future.

CXXXII.

Topaz Internment Camp:
Central Utah, The Beehive State.
Confinement stings.
The *Topaz Times* and *Trek*,
Not an enterprising voyage,
Seeking a distant star. Explorers
Waylaid in barbed-wire detention.
It should never happen here.

CXXXIII.

Colorado River (Poston) Internment Camp:
Arizona. Heat and tears.
Roasten, Toastin, and Dustin.
Hopes and tomorrows melted here.
To what end. White man's fear?
Three miles from the river.
Three miles from desert refreshment.
When the sun set, nobody saw me cry.

CXXXIV.

Gila River Internment Camp:
Near Phoenix. Dry river beds,
No reborn birds. Baseball was a savior.
America's pastime. A field, a ball.
Legs running until the sun died.
A single watchtower, though
The desert was not a friend.
Apologies finally granted.

CXXXV.

Granada (Amache) Internment Camp:
Colorado. Rocky Mountain Lows.
National Register of Historic Places.
Historic or oneiric?
Like sand blown away in the wind.
The smallest camp by population,
High prairie beset by desolation,
Or in the morning light: my penance.

CXXXVI.

Jerome Internment Camp:
Arkansas, echoes of enslavement linger.
The last camp to concentrate wrongdoing,
The first to close. May the doors
Be thrown to the
Bottom of the Mississippi.
Along with racial segregation,
And loyalty questionnaires.

CXXXVII.

Manzanar Internment Camp:
California. Barracks of shame
In the shadow of the Sierra Nevada.
Another place where Native Americans,
First occupied, tread, died.
Where the new Americans,
My adopted people who settled
Built more buildings, but many walls.

CXXXVIII.

Minidoka Internment Camp:
Idaho. Just north of Eden,
But far from it.
Snakes of dread put citizens
Near the Snake River,
Thirty-six blocks of barracks.
Friends of Minidoka,
I honor your role.

CXXXIX.

Rohwer Internment Camp:
Arkansas. Another place in
Dixie. Dreams die.
Freedom lies.
There are no winners.
Just guards and hate,
While some try to love.
Where's the Mississippi?

CXL.

Tule Lake Internment Camp:
California. The most humans,
Humans who shared red blood,
Fear turned into acts of racism,
Turned into a National Monument.
United States v. Masaaki Kuwabara.
Mr. Kuwabara, and others, fought
For their rights: Due process, sir.

CXLI.

Hiroshima:
The injustice of all.
I am the instigator.
I am a destroyer of worlds.
End the war?
It wasn't a military target.
The melted faces haunt me.
The Dome, cranes of peace, forgive me.

CXLII.

Nagasaki:
Three days later.
I repeat the sin.
Peaceful town.
No need. No cause.
No words. No compassion.
I beseech my children.
Never again.

CXLIII.

Exoneration:
What words can I say?
What sounds can I preserve?
What apology is good enough?
What peace can be served?
What rivers flow to where
The residue of democracy
Tries to rise again?

CXLIV.

The Little Big Horn:
George Armstrong Custer.
Last in his West Point class.
Gettysburg, present at Appomattox.
Do not celebrate his death.
The fury spawned.
The land revoked.
The land the Earth always owned.

CXLV.

The Counted:
The dearly departed remembered.
Census Bureau not a Politburo.
Every American voice,
All of my children. Exalt.
Do not execute righteous action.
There are more people
That need to be accounted for.

CXLVI.

Peace & Love
Do not bow to law and order;
They abolish its need,
Render these things obsolete:
The strict hand, the belt.
Systems of control break
When the light is absent.
Do the right thing. We'll shine.

CXLVII.

System of Government
Popular Vote Wins the Election.
Plain and simple.
No faithless electors.
No meaningless votes.
Raise the action. The pot stirs,
Melting no more, freed
From electoral poison.

CXLVIII.

Climate Change:
Hurricane Alley became
Hurricane Boulevard.
Did the weathermen inject humor?
Fossils fuel pollution,
Men in office too long.
Oil spills less antidotes,
Everyone witness Earth's rage.

CXLIX.

Turtle Island:
A vast utopia, destined, adorned.
I know this name. Another world.
Satellites launched in my name
See the glory, the fertile creatures.
I grant them to those who care,
The guardians of the environment,
The indigenous whisperers on the land.

CL.

McDonald's:
Over 100 billion burgers served.
Cultural imperialism at its finest:
Mickey D's steps from the Kremlin.
Happy Meals and movie tie-ins.
Ronald McDonald, Hamburglar.
Kroc stole the show. Capitalism.
This isn't my best face.

CLI.

Limiting Interest of Spouses of Beneficiaries:
If the spouses of those benefitting
From the divvying do not adhere
To the Constitution, to the idea of equals,
Or conspire to suppress votes,
Spew hateful rhetoric or fascism,
Attacking the press. They get nothing.

CLII.

Trustee Compensation in Advance:
Trustees, they are not to be paid,
There is no inherent good in paying
Those who are already in a position
To become Trustees. Let the
Weakest and poorest among
My survivors, my children,
My citizens reap the benefits.

CLIII.

Guardians of Children:
Cages are meant for real
Criminals, real felony crimes.
Not prisons for the poor,
Searching El Norte for more.
The youngest among us
Are seeds for tomorrow.
I demand they are treated well.

CLIV.

Coalition of the Willing:
These words must not be uttered
In reference to war or
The spoils of oil.
In fact, they shouldn't be used
At all. Paradigm shift.
There is no need for willing
Citizens if action is just.

CLV.

Antarctic Claims:
I relinquish all claims
To the Southern Continent.
It belongs to the world.
Its water will save us,
Or if fought over, will
Be our undoing.
Do not fight over water.

CLVI.

Arctic Claims:
The natural gas, in native
Lands. It is not ours for the taking.
Transcend. Find new energy.
Clean, unrelenting, unending.
Without raping Mother Earth.
Without leading to greater doom.
Those who come after, I beg you.

CLVII.

Non-contestability of Bequests:
If anyone challenges my bequests,
They will receive nothing.
The bequests are set forth
As dictated. *My* wishes:
They cannot be changed,
Even by Trustees. I hope for heirs.
If I die, other nations may have too.

CLVIII.

Eligibility:
Citizens of the world,
You are all Americans.
We are all Earthlings.
You are—hopefully—still here.
Everyone who defends reason.
By protecting votes and the Bill of Rights.
There is no such thing as three-fifths.

CLIX.

Police Brutality I:
New rules for a new day.
No pensions for dirty cops.
Excessive force, no pay,
Turn the other cheek
Works the other way.
Your pay gets donated to those
You've animalized, sent to a grave.

CLX.

Police Brutality II:
Yesterday is gone.
Tomorrow, your penance.
Listen to the cries of the slain
In a room. Press play.
What if it was your son?
What if it was your daughter?
Who will march for you?

CLXI.

Artificial Intelligence:
A computer will analyze
This poem in the future.
Distant? Or in 10 minutes?
Or perhaps 10 years?
Whatever it says I hope
It's infused with humanity,
Foresight, wisdom.

CLXII.

Space Force:
Do not export
The worst parts
Of my democratic ideas.
The Electoral College,
Gerrymandering,
Voter suppression.
Seed the stars with justice.

CLXIII.

Racism:
Do not divide and conquer
With boasts of superiority.
I was built on it, but it leads
To my untimely demise.
Teach the children to love.
Teach the highest morals.
Hate is an acquired education.

CLXIV.

Recidivism:
Poverty makes us all poor.
Invest in people;
In their futures.
Not the sins of their past.
Make clear the gateway,
External factors as broken dams.
Build greater public works.

CLXV.

Kakistocracy:
If nothing else is followed,
If nothing else is learned.
Do not let the worst rule.
Fascism is not welcome.
A basic knowledge of the
Constitution? Federal statutes?
Is that too much to ask?

CLXVI.

Gun Control:
The Second Amendment
Shouldn't mean becoming
A vigilante and killing
Two people on the streets
Of Kenosha. Guns kill people,
And people kill people.
I implore common sense laws.

CLXVII.

FISA:
Foreign.
Intelligence.
Surveillance.
Act. React.
This is not right.
This is not left.
This is an erosion.

CLXVIII.

Vote:
Not voting is a threat.
Voting for the dark
Side is a threat.
The Electoral College
Is a world threat.
Suppression is a threat.
Voting is not.

CLXIX.

Arlington National Cemetery:
Privileges extend to all.
All born and bred from Kenya,
Born and bred of Earth.
Human voices, human cries.
Birthed of truth and human dignity.
Do not desecrate. Respect the fallen.
A scourge will suffice in my wake.

CLXX.

Library of Congress:
The holdings of this great
Temple of learning,
Shall be made available
To all, regardless of nation.
Let knowledge guide us
Toward peace. Intelligence
Is the antidote to fear.

CLXXI.

National Archives:
Another repository
Of faithful diligence.
Keep her mighty,
Keep her grace.
The sounds of NASA,
The images of the past,
Echoing in the future.

CLXXII.

The Declaration of Independence:
Philadelphia, July 4, 1776.
Almighty ideas. Blighted.
We were not created equal
When these notions found ink.
Enslaved Africans did not
Have unalienable rights. Dream harder.

CLXXIII.

The Constitution:
Will not enforce itself.
Remember these words.
Heed this warning.
The Constitution
Is only as good as the
People abiding by it.
Silence is complicity.

CLXXIV.

The Preamble:
Pray tell the division.
The disassembly of
Words on papyrus.
My wish is that
Many planets and federations
Examine this document,
Amble ably on.

CLXXV.

Article One:
A House, a Senate.
Established, Terms,
Ten Sections.
An Army, a Navy,
The Post Office,
Section 8, not a
Conduct discharge.

CLXXVI.

Article Two:
Natural-born eligibility.
Let's revisit conditions,
Presidential ambition.
If *birtherism* is your bag,
You are ineligible.
This is my interpretation.
This is not law; it should be.

CLXXVII.

Article Three:
Treason?
The American public
Knows it when it sees it.
Russia, if you're listening...
Seeking power from without.
It seems simple enough.
That's what I'm hearing.

CLXXVIII.

Article Four:
A Republican
Form of government.
Can we get a new name?
New states, not references
To a Deep State.
We aspire to one state:
Freedom.

CLXXIX.

Article Five:
My most cherished
Tenet. Like a
Child's broken toy,
We can fix it.
Amendments.
The great forgiving,
The eternal remixing.

CLXXX.

Article Six:
No religious test.
Do not test this.
Fundamentalism
At each end
Has bad ends.
My supremacy litmus:
The Constitution.

CLXXXI.

Article Seven:
Unanimous Consent.
I want all to be true.
I want all to adhere
To the noble principles,
Tried, and without lies.
I want the words
To keep eternal meaning.

CLXXXII.

First Amendment:
The media is not the enemy.
It is the institution
Saving this institution:
Say what you will.
Peaceful assembly,
Not harassing protestors
And instigating violence.

CLXXXIII.

Second Amendment:
Well regulated.
Well, regulated
We'll regulate.
Will regulated.
Regulated, well.
Regulated well.
Regulated, we'll...

CLXXXIV.

Third Amendment:
In a manner prescribed
By law. What law
Would that be?
The Patriot Act?
The wiggle room
Is inherently unruly.
No quartered soldiers.

CLXXXV.

Fourth Amendment:
Where's the warrant?
The paper we need?
What happens when
A corrupt judge
Issues it corruptly?
Justice or something else?
Let not me bleed.

CLXXXVI.

Fifth Amendment:
Processed and due.
Double jeopardy
Isn't an incriminating game.
Private property
Untaken without
Compensation.
Beware eminent domain.

CLXXXVII.

Sixth Amendment:
Speedy, public, impartial.
A trial and a trail of rights.
We must always denote
The nature of the charge
And cause of the accusation.
Witnesses for and against.
You will have counsel.

CLXXXVIII.

Seventh Amendment:
I will not have $20
In my pocket after
The proceeds and the
Purses and the spoils
Of war are dispersed.
Still give me a peace,
A willing trial by jury.

CLXXXIX

Eighth Amendment:
I will not stand for
Cruel and unusual
Punishments:
Waterboarding, torture.
Sit these sins out.
Excise them from mind.
No fines paid, only mine.

CXC.

Ninth Amendment:
The rights of the People
Shall not be denied.
Individuals can breathe,
Can sing, can disparage
My sins, but their rights
Remain. Government
Is always the People.

CXCI.

Tenth Amendment:
Marriage, divorce, adoption.
Among the powers reserved
To the states or the People,
The federal government
Only those specifically
Granted by the Constitution.
Commerce within each state.

CXCII.

Eleventh Amendment:
Power suits and lawsuits.
States do not have to hear
A suit if it's based on
Federal law. The jury
Is still out. My Trustees,
Will a state's immunity
In state court hold?

CXCIII.

Twelfth Amendment:
What a convoluted
Solution to an unequal
Situation. One vote
Means nothing in
This penurious system.
One more time with feeling:
Abolish the Electoral College.

CXCIV.

Thirteenth Amendment:
December 6, 1865. Lucky 13.
Thirteen ways to right an infinite wrong.
If the Constitution lives and breathes,
Why was the 13th needed at all?
Weren't we all equal under the sun,
From the country's first light?
Black Codes: Hell no.

CXCV.

Fourteenth Amendment:
A new threshold: If insurrection against
A fascist leader is necessary,
Only 46 percent of each
House is needed to remove
The disability of any
Person who participated
From attaining higher office.

CXCVI.

Fifteenth Amendment:
"The right of Citizens of
The United States to vote
Shall not be denied or abridged
By the United States or by any
State on account of race, color,
Or previous condition of servitude."
Congress, enforce it.

CXCVII.

Sixteenth Amendment:
"Without regard to any
Census or enumeration."
The tax collector is coming.
Matthew was a collector,
A disciple in another book.
Make sure it's put to good use.
Don't spend it all in one place.

CXCVIII.

Seventeenth Amendment:
I propose a tweak,
A nudge, a nodding change:
Term limits for Senators.
Three cycles, 18 years,
Then turn over the leaves,
Bury your tears.
Buy our own insurance.

CXCIX.

Eighteenth Amendment:
Inebriation? Prohibition!
Who ginned this up?
Good in theory.
Good for the bowels.
But who needs debauchery,
Wine and sins, if the
Amendments come correct?

CC.

Nineteenth Amendment:
My daughters can vote.
My daughters can lead.
My daughters can combat
Climate change, cancer,
Cancerous leaders,
Siphoning love, sowing hostility.
My daughters will be President.

CCI.

Twentieth Amendment:
Congress will meet much
More than at least
Once per year.
This is my vow.
Jan. 20, darkness at noon?
What recompense?
When the emperor has no pants.

CCII.

Twenty-First Amendment:
The Hangover. Your societal debt
Hangs over us all. Pay your tithe.
Revel in gallant liquid courage.
I think we can agree.
A modicum of fun,
A glass clinked in moderation.
Don't drink; I'll drive.

CCIII.

Twenty-Second Amendment:
No presidents elected more
Than twice. See, I can be nice.
Or if you're warming
Someone else's seat for more
Than two years, you can
Only be elected once.
This may stave Civil War one day.

CCIV.

Twenty-Third Amendment:
Taxation Without Representation.
The District, the unjust status.
Trustees, change D.C.'s game.
Two senators, and a representative.
If the monuments and memorials
Are gone. If the city's not radioactive.
If the Constitution isn't underground.

CCV.

Twenty-Fourth Amendment:
Voting. Here we are again.
A simple task, but always
Battles, always tanks,
Always nuclear weapons
In the name of suppression.
No poll tax or other taxes.
But count the chads.

CCVI.

Twenty-Fifth Amendment:
Emoluments. Act fast.
The president is unable
To perform the duties of
His office. Don't let
Him lie about that.
Shooting someone on Fifth
Avenue is not a joke.

CCVII.

Twenty-Sixth Amendment:
And yes, as predicted,
We haven't seen the last
Of this dear friend, the
Bulwark of my time
On this planet. Legitimate.
Eighteen years is what you need,
Eighteen tears exercise action.

CCVIII.

Twenty-Seventh Amendment:
Congress is a public privilege.
Service should be free.
Everyone should have their
Health care system,
That is among this dying country's
Greatest wishes. No pay raises
Until the Electoral College is gone.

CCIX

Closing Endorsements:
John Hancock, the vanity,
Reminds me of another vain man,
The clearer of crowds. The Big
Man clutching a Bible in front
Of a church, for all the world to see.
In facts we trust. In the hopes
The Constitution doesn't break.

CCX.

Dissolution of the Contract:
The unspoken, uncolored
Contract writhes upon my death.
Freedom of speech, writ of
Habeas corpus, long ago ideas.
Fanciful citizens await release.
Free to fire guns at will.
On a planet of corpses.

CCXI.

The House Un-American Activities Committee:
Dalton Trumbo would write it better.
I, the United States, call for an immediate
Reconvening of HUAC with this purview:
Anyone who suppresses votes,
Asks Russia if they're listening,
Attacks freedom of speech, flaunts
Emoluments, will be subpoenaed forthwith.

CCXII.

The New America I:
Addendum to the Contract.
If you're reading this, I'm dead.
This is the superseding law.
My dominance is my will.
We will walk together again,
In a new land, hand in hand,
Across a Selma bridge renamed.

CCXIII.

The New America II:
Rise up. Overcome.
You won't have to pay decades
For things you need today.
The beaches will overflow.
The sands will consume.
Divest and reinvest.
Reinvent the wheel.

CCXIV.

The New America III:
Breathe new life into barren lands.
Wind. Solar. Desalination plants.
The power of the tides.
Divine energy. Clean.
Provides infinite jobs too.
The transfer to a new system,
Then the maintenance of robots.

CCXV.

The New America IV:
Facts matter. Truth.
Science, go to bat,
You're the new pastime.
Played on fields of dreams.
Beakers, nanotech, atoms.
Experiments verified,
Results on demand.

CCXVI.

The New America V:
Green technology brings green.
Green fields, green trees,
Greenbacks and greener pastures.
Not green with envy.
Everyone will have plenty.
We are all ushers of the globe,
Bringing forth a sustainable world.

CCXVII.

The New America VI:
Martial law, Marshall's call.
Riot police and rioters.
Cameras at the ready.
Is this the past, present, future?
No more bloodshed.
Can one nation do it all?
Images must not trump reason.

CCXVIII.

The New America VII:
Stadiums filled with
The screams, not of fans,
But the triumphant hands
Pulling a lever for the first time.
Uptown, Downtown, all around.
LeBron and CP3.
Young people I beseech thee.

CCXIX.

The New America VIII:
Oxford commas, exclamation
Points, the weapons of
Demarcation in the bowels
Of a new nation, rising
Like the mythological bird.
New Atlantis, new technology.
New, new, new.

CCXX.

The New America IX:
There will be new wrongs, righted,
New rights, wronged, new things,
All out of sight. Then fixed.
When they arise I want them to
Sing organically, together,
In harmony, no trepidation.
We are one nation.

CCXXI.

The New America X:
Seven shots. Not again.
41 shots. Not again.
I can't breathe. Not again.
A foot on the neck. Not again.
An African-American man
Is threatening me. Not again.
Two justice systems. No more.

CCXXII.

Final Words:
I am the United States of America.
I may be dead, but I am not defeated.
Defiant, like Maya says, I rise.
I stand tall, sing a new anthem.
Legislative, judicial, executive.
Branches of a living tree
With roots in humanity's breeze.

OTHER WORK BY KELVIN C. BIAS

MILKMAN (Novel)

What happens when everyman Calder Boyd starts to lactate? The Manhattanite becomes a media cause célèbre nicknamed the Milkman and old and new problems spill forth. The son of a former NBA star and a Norwegian artist, Calder copes with his strained marriage, losing his copywriting job at a boutique ad agency, a male-empowerment espousing mailman and a porn-star performance artist who wants to exploit him. He also deals with his late father's legacy and his wife's past indiscretion—all while breastfeeding their newborn daughter. Calder eventually becomes a pawn in the battle between a feminist organization and a militant men's society as he tries to become a better husband and man. The Fourth Estate, sex, art, love, memory, marriage and family converge during the snowiest winter on record in this commentary on contemporary American fatherhood.

WHISPERS OF A DYING SUN (Poetry)

These poems represent the vestiges of man from the perspective of a distant future. Akin to radio signals, the remnants of humanity streak toward a black hole where art, politics, love, technology, philosophy, science and the yearning for eternity accrete. Prophetic, stoic, polyphasic, the words disassemble and recombine on the other side in search of a new sun. I hope these poems find a closer home in your personal universe, heard but you're unsure of their origin, like whispers.

SEXOPOLIS: POEMS ON LOVE AND SEX

Love is a liberation, an act, a rebellion, a restriction, a communion. This poetry collection covers the universal topics of love and sex. From erotic to platonic and from marital to familial, love comes in many forms. We don't always get it, but we all crave it.

IMMACULATE DUST: LOVE POEMS

This poetry collection delves headlong into the world of love. Encompassing the realms of dream, fantasy and reality, the poems intend to engender not just love, but more pointedly, lovemaking. Lust. Love. Languor. These are three states of mind and body before, during and after the most pleasant poetry of human interaction: consented sex. We all possess desire and we are all made of dust. Immaculate dust.

21 PARTICLES OF ETERNITY (Poetry)

Is eternity a quantifiable entity? An existence that can be divided into smaller particles, assembled and disassembled like a puzzle? Can it be bent? Borrowed? Recycled? Eternity is elusive. It constantly seems beyond our grasp yet always within our reach. *21 Particles of Eternity* covers topics as disparate as Mars and pornography, and ranging from global warming and parenthood to politics and death. The poet posits this: perhaps there are hidden portals where eternity can be glimpsed for fleeting moments, and the quest to find them brings meaning. How many particles will you find?

IF THE SKY IS AWAKE (Poetry)

Why do we have a 24-hour day, 60-minute hour, and 60-second minute?
Thank the ancient Egyptians, Sumerians and Babylonians. Going further
back, in humanity's early days, time was simply measured by the interval
between sunrise and sunset. Today, we have much more precise methods.
One second is defined as the duration of 9,192,631,770 periods of the
radiation corresponding to the transition between the two hyperfine levels
of the ground state of a cesium 133 atom. *Confusing?* Yes. Sometimes what
transpires in daylight is the purest. Each day is a new dawn, a chance to
reinvent yourself, find new love, rekindle an old one, and peer into the sky
and feel awake. Reading poetry is like living life by your own clock. Lose
yourself in your own sky.

ABOUT THE AUTHOR

Kelvin C. Bias is a journalist, novelist, poet, filmmaker, and raconteur. However, his most important moniker is father. He holds a B.A. in Political Science from the University of Arizona and an M.F.A in Screenwriting from NYU. He lives in New York City with his family.

The Last Will & Testament of the United States of America is his sixth poetry collection. Connect with Kelvin on Instagram & Twitter: @archivezero

www.ingramcontent.com/pod-product-compliance
Lightning Source LLC
Chambersburg PA
CBHW072356090426
42741CB00012B/3049